FIRST AMERICANS
The Tlingit

SARAH De CAPUA

Marshall Cavendish
Benchmark
New York

ACKNOWLEDGMENTS

Series consultant: Raymond Bial

Marshall Cavendish Benchmark
99 White Plains Road
Tarrytown, New York 10591
www.marshallcavendish.us

All Internet sites were available and accurate when sent to press.
The game on page 21 comes from the Alaska Native Knowledge Network (http://www.ankn.uaf.edu).
The recipe on page 23 comes from NativeTech (http://www.nativetech.org/recipes).

Library of Congress Cataloging-in-Publication Data
De Capua, Sarah.
The Tlingit / by Sarah De Capua.
p. cm. — (First Americans)
Includes bibliographical references and index.
Summary: "Provides comprehensive information on the background, lifestyle, beliefs,
and present-day lives of the Tlingit people"—Provided by publisher.
ISBN 978-0-7614-4135-9
1. Tlingit Indians—History—Juvenile literature. 2. Tlingit Indians—Social life and customs—Juvenile literature. I. Title.
E99.T6D37 2010
979.8004'9727—dc22
2008041179

Front cover: A Tlingit boy wears a traditional button blanket and headdress for a dance at Saxman Village, Alaska.
Title page: A Tlingit Chilkat weaving made of mountain goat wool and caribou skin, displayed at Chicago's Field Museum of Natural History
Photo research by: Connie Gardner
Cover photo by Vance Stream/Corbis

The photographs in this book are used by permission and through the courtesy of: The photographs in this book are used by permission and through the courtesy of: *Art Resource*: Werner Forman, 1; *Getty Images*: David Job, 4; Don Klumpp, 26; *Corbis*: Stuart Westmorland, 6; Poodle Rock, 12; Tom Bean, 14; Vance Stream, 19; James Marshall, 20; Werner Forman, 22; Museum of History and Industry, 32; *Nativestock*: Marilyn "Angel" Wynn, 16, 39; *Granger Collection*: 28; *Alamy*: Purcell Team, 8; Northwind, 10; *Bridgeman*: A Bridal Group by John Andrea and Son, Edward Sheriff Curtis, 30; *AP Photo*: Seanna O'Sullivan, 34, 36; Chris Miller, 41.

Editor: Deborah Grahame
Publisher: Michelle Bisson
Art Director: Anahid Hamparian
Series Designer: Symon Chow

Printed in Malaysia
1 3 5 6 4 2

CONTENTS

1 · WHO ARE THE TLINGIT PEOPLE?

The Tlingit (pronounced KLINK-it) people live in villages in southeastern Alaska. They also live on **reserves** in British Columbia and Yukon Territory in Canada. Some Tlingit live beside their non-Native neighbors in other parts of the United States and Canada. There are about 15,000 Tlingit in the United States. An additional 1,200 Tlingit live in Canada.

The Tlingit call themselves *Lingít*, which means "people." They are also known as the Kolosh. Their culture is closely related to that of the Haida native people. The Haida also live in southeastern Alaska and western Canada.

Thousands of years ago large sheets of ice called glaciers covered the land. People probably reached present-day Alaska by crossing a land bridge from what is now Russia. Among them were **ancestors** of the Tlingit. Traditional Tlingit territory includes the Alaskan **Panhandle** and western Canada.

A view of southeastern Alaska's Mendenhall Glacier, which is located on traditional Tlingit lands

Humpback whales feeding in the waters of the Inside Passage

The Tlingit of western Canada are known as inland Tlingit.

Alaska's Panhandle includes many islands. The Panhandle is covered by rain forests of cedar, spruce, fir, and hemlock trees. The waters between the islands and the mainland are called the Inside Passage. The waters are fairly warm and the climate is mild. The waters abound with fish, including salmon and halibut, and shellfish such as clams. They provide food for seals, sea lions, sea otters, killer whales (orcas), and

Tlingit Traditional Territory

YUKON
TERRITORY

Juneau

Taku River

GULF OF

ALASKA

Sitka   Kake

BRITISH
COLUMBIA

Ketchikan

Tongass
National
Forest

This map shows the traditional homeland of the Tlingit.

This Tlingit canoe is decorated with an eagle.

porpoises. Bears, deer, and many small mammals live on the islands and mainland. All of these animals provided food, oil, clothing, and other materials for the Tlingit. The forests provided wood for fuel and for building houses. Tree bark and tree roots were also used to make clothing.

The Tlingit traded fish, **game**, and furs with fellow Tlingit and other Native people who lived along the coast. The Tlingit traveled from one village to another in huge dug-out canoes made of cedar.

The first contact between Tlingit people and non-Native people probably occurred in the 1600s. This is when Russians began to trade with the Tlingit. The Russians gave the Tlingit tools, wool blankets, and other supplies. The Tlingit gave the Russians otter furs, and the Russians sold the furs in China.

Carving a Canoe

The sea has always been the chief source of food for the Tlingit. Long ago small canoes carried them to hunting or fishing areas. Large canoes were used to travel on long trading trips, to go to special feasts, or to go to war.

Many men made a canoe, but they were directed by an especially skilled carver. The carver chose the men who went into the forest and chopped down the cedar tree with axes. The tree's branches were cut off. Then the men chopped a hole in one side of the log. Next they built a small fire in the hole and let it burn. Then they put out the fire and dug out the ashes. They repeated these steps of burning and digging until there was enough room for people to sit inside the log.

When the canoe was finished, family symbols such as birds were painted in bright colors on its sides. Canoes with high bows, or fronts, were made to cut through high ocean waves. Canoes with flat bottoms were used to travel along streams. The largest canoes were freight canoes. They carried large loads, such as salmon, from a fishing camp to a village.

Tlingit canoes were between 30 and 70 feet (9 and 21 meters) long. Some were as wide as 7 feet (2 m). The largest and widest canoes could hold twenty people or carry as much as 5 tons (4,500 kilograms) of cargo. Today's Tlingit still carve canoes, but most fishing families travel in modern boats that have motors.

The fur trade between the Tlingit and the Russians was mostly peaceful. The Russians did not settle permanently in the area, so the Tlingit did not think their territory was threatened.

In the 1700s a Danish explorer named Vitus Bering arrived in Alaska. Bering was sent by the czar, or ruler, of Russia. Bering claimed all of the land for Russia. Soon after, Russian fur traders settled permanently in Alaska. They built trading forts and set up communities. The Tlingit did not

Some of Vitus Bering's ships were wrecked in Alaska's coastal waters in 1741.

like the newcomers, who took away their land and introduced unfamiliar customs. Tensions between the Tlingit and Russians led to fighting.

In 1778 British explorer Captain James Cook arrived off the coast of Alaska. He wanted British trading companies to make money from the fur trade in China. Word of the large amounts of money being made in the fur trade reached Spanish and American traders, too. A tidal wave of traders soon came to the region. Besides tools and blankets, they traded flour, sugar, guns, and sails for Tlingit canoes and otter furs.

Russian, European, and American traders carried diseases such as measles, smallpox, and influenza (the flu). The Tlingit and their Native neighbors had never encountered these diseases. Their bodies had no natural defenses against them. As a result the diseases spread quickly throughout the Native communities. Hundreds became sick and died.

Meanwhile Russia had kept control of Alaska. But in 1867 Russia sold Alaska to the United States. In the 1870s gold was discovered in southeastern Alaska. Thousands of people rushed

Captain James Cook

to the region to mine the gold. **Missionaries** arrived too. They built churches and schools. The U.S. government also built schools.

By the late 1800s and early 1900s, it was difficult for the Tlingit to live on their traditional lands and follow their own way of life. The U.S. government did not allow them to make money from the fish, trees, gold, and other resources that were taken from their lands. Inland Tlingit experienced the same treatment from the Canadian government. Some Native groups signed treaties with the United States. They agreed to move onto **reservations**. However, the Tlingit in Alaska refused to sign a treaty. They stayed in small communities along Alaska's coast. The Tlingit in Canada eventually agreed to move to a reserve. The way of life for the Tlingit along Alaska's coast and in western Canada had been changed forever.

Katlian and the Iron People

Katlian (or K'alyáan) was a Tlingit chief in the early 1800s, during the days of the Russian fur trade. The Tlingit called the Russians "Iron People" because of the iron cannonballs they used in battle. In 1802 Katlian's nephew fell in love with the daughter of a Russian trader. When the nephew tried to steal the young woman so he could marry her, the girl's father killed him. In revenge Katlian killed the son of a trader. Alexandr Baranov, the governor of the Russian settlement, ordered Katlian to turn himself in so the Russians could arrest him. Katlian refused. Instead he inspired the Tlingit to fight the Russians. The Tlingit and Russians fought a four-day battle. Both sides used guns, cannons, and other weapons. Many Tlingit and Russians were killed. But the Tlingit fought on under Katlian's brave leadership. According to Tlingit history, Baranov surrendered to Katlian. Baranov then brought the Tlingit food, clothing, and other supplies. Katlian became a hero to his people. A U.S. Navy ship that sailed from 1940 to 1947 was named for him.

2 · LIFE IN SOUTHEASTERN ALASKA

The ancestors of today's Tlingit people lived farther north than any other southeastern Native Alaskan group. The Tlingit were organized into family groups called clans. There were two clans: Yeil (Raven) and Ch'aak (Eagle). Sometimes the name Gooch (Wolf) is used instead of Eagle. Although the members of a clan were not always related by blood, they considered themselves brothers and sisters.

Tlingit villages were headed by chiefs. The villages were made up of large houses that were made of cedar. Several families lived together in one house. Sometimes as many as one hundred people lived in a single house. Some villages had only one house. The largest villages had as many as forty houses. Most villages, however, had about ten houses.

The Tlingit's houses were called plankhouses. They got this name because they were made of flat boards called planks.

A totem pole sits outside a brightly decorated Tlingit clan house at a state park in Ketchikan, Alaska.

Cedar was used because it splits easily. Builders made rectangular frames with cedar logs. Then planks were used for the walls, roof, and floor.

Plankhouses were built in rows. The entrance of each home faced the water. Plankhouses had no windows. The Tlingit painted their houses with colorful pictures of animals such as birds and fish.

A traditional Tlingit cedar plank longhouse constructed at the Alaska Native Heritage Center in Anchorage

Inside the house, mats were hung from the ceiling to divide the houses into private spaces for each family. These mats were made of woven cedar bark. A large fire pit for cooking was made in the center of the floor. Roof planks were raised and lowered with long poles to let the smoke from the cooking fire escape. The planks were lowered to keep the water out when it rained.

Some Tlingit carved animals into the wooden posts that supported the houses. They also made carvings in doorways and entrances. Tall wooden carvings called totem poles stood in front of the houses. Some totem poles were more than 20 feet (6 m) high. They were carved with figures of birds or animals that represented a family or a clan. The figures were then painted in bright colors. Totem poles recorded the history of a family or a clan. Some totem poles recorded the achievements of a village chief.

After a totem pole was raised, a ceremony was held. A respected member of the family or clan would tell the story of the figures carved into the pole. In many Tlingit communities today, visitors can see beautiful totem poles and carvings on plankhouses.

In spring and fall the Tlingit set up camps where they could fish. They also gathered berries and plants for food. Camp houses usually looked like small plankhouses. Like plankhouses, they were made of cedar.

The Tlingit became well known for their arts. Tlingit women wove blankets, mats, and baskets out of cedar bark and the long grasses that grew along the coast. Men carved wood into totem poles, tools, masks, and boxes used for cooking and storage. The Tlingit also carved and painted dishes, weapons, and fishhooks.

Tlingit men hunted land animals such as deer, bears, caribou, mountain goats, and mountain sheep. They fished for salmon, halibut, and eulachon (or candlefish). They gathered clams and mussels when the tide went out. They hunted sea animals, including seals, sea lions, otters, and killer whales (orcas). Men also cut down trees and made planks for the houses.

Tlingit women gathered forest plants, bird eggs, and

A Tlingit dancer displays a blanket decorated with an eagle outlined in buttons.

berries. In addition to weaving, women also did the cooking and made clothing.

Children learned the Tlingit way of life by watching and helping adults. Tlingit children did not go to school. Boys learned to hunt, fish, and carve from their fathers. Girls learned by helping their mothers.

Before the arrival of foreign traders, Tlingit clothing was

These salmon are being dried outdoors using the same method that Alaska's southeast coastal Native people have used for centuries.

made from the inner bark of cedar trees. Cedar trees have two layers of bark. The hard, outer bark was used for items such as bowls, plates, and tools. Narrow strips of outer bark were used as string on which fish were hung to dry. Dried fish was stored to eat later. The inner bark was soft. Women shredded it by hand or by placing the bark on a large rock and pressing a small rock along its length until it separated into strips. The strips were woven into skirts and capes for women. Men wore leggings made from seal skin or deerskin. Sometimes strips

Jackstraws

Village life kept the Tlingit busy. But they still had time to play games.

Materials: Bunch of slender sticks and a wooden hook for each player

Players: Any number

How to Play: A player grasps the bunch of sticks between the thumb and forefinger, resting one end of the sticks on the floor. The player releases the sticks, letting them fall in a small heap. Each player then uses the hook to pick up as many sticks as he or she can, without moving any of the sticks except the one on the hook. Each player keeps the sticks he or she has removed. The player who has the most sticks when the heap is gone is the winner.

were shredded many times, until only stringlike strands remained. These strands were woven into diapers, towels, and fringe to decorate blankets and clothing.

Clothing was often dyed in different colors. The most common colors were red and black. The Tlingit wore moccasins made of woven bark or tree roots. They also wore hats made of roots. Sometimes the hats were trimmed with sea otter fur. Clothing was covered in whale oil to make it waterproof. Ceremonial dress included carved masks, weapons, and colorful robes. Some robes, called Chilkat robes, were trimmed with animal fur and fringe. Men and women wore earrings and nose rings. Some had tattoos or wore disks that pierced their lower lip.

Chilkat robe

Salmon Patties

Salmon has always been the most important food in the Tlingit diet. Although this recipe contains ingredients that were not available to the Tlingit of long ago, it was created by a Tlingit cook. Ask an adult to help you. Always wash your hands with soap and water before you begin.

Ingredients

- 1 pound (450 grams) fresh salmon or canned salmon, drained
- 1 egg
- 1/3 (85 milliliters) cup diced onion
- 1/4 (60 ml) cup bread crumbs
- Pinch of pepper
- 2 tablespoons (30 ml) minced pimento
- 3 tablespoons (45 ml) diced chives
- 1/2 (125 ml) cup flour
- 1/2 (125 ml) cup cornmeal
- Pinch of salt (optional)

Coat a frying pan with cooking oil, such as canola or extra virgin olive oil. Set the frying pan over medium heat. In a bowl, combine salmon, egg, onion, bread crumbs, pepper, pimento, and chives. Measure the mixture into 1/4- to 1/2-cup (60- to 125-ml) portions. Flatten into patties no thicker than 3/4 inch (1.5 centimeters). Spread flour and cornmeal onto a plate and mix them together. Coat the patties on both sides in the flour/cornmeal mixture. Fry patties in hot oil until they are golden brown. (If the salmon is canned, the frying time will be only a few minutes because the salmon is already cooked.) Salt to taste. Serve with rice or green salad.

Tlingit Craft: Painted Wooden Box

The Tlingit were skilled craftspeople. They carved and decorated wooden boxes for a variety of uses, including cooking and storage.

You will need:

- Brown paper bag
- Wooden box (You can buy wooden boxes in a variety of sizes at any craft or hobby store.)
- Paintbrushes
- Paints in any colors you choose (Favorite colors among the Tlingit are red and black.)
- Pencil (optional)

1. Cut the brown paper bag along one side. Cut off the bottom. Spread the bag flat on your work surface to protect the surface from spills.

2. Paint your wooden box. Decorate it with pictures and symbols that are meaningful to you. Do you like to fish? Paint fish on your box. Do you have a pet dog, cat, or bird? Paint a picture of your pet. Be creative. You can paint any animal, person, or thing on your box.

(See examples, below.) You may find it helpful to draw pictures on your box in pencil first, then paint over them.

3. When you are finished painting your box, allow it to dry. This may take several hours. Be sure to clean your paintbrushes and store your paints properly, so you can use them on other projects—or maybe to paint another box.

Show your wooden box to others and share what you have learned about the Tlingit.

3 · TLINGIT BELIEFS

Today most Tlingit are Christians, although many people combine their Christian religion with traditional beliefs. Tlingit beliefs centered on the Creator, who was called Kah-shu-goon-yah. The Creator made the world. Raven was another important figure in Tlingit religion. Raven was said to have created people and placed the land, waters, and air where they are now. Raven was also said to have started many Tlingit customs.

The Tlingit also believed that spirits called *jek* lived in nature—in the land, rivers, ocean, forests, and plants. Spirits also lived in the sun, moon, and stars. The spirits had powers to help or hurt the Tlingit. In order to receive the spirits' help, the Tlingit performed **rituals** to please them. Ceremonies to give thanks to the spirits followed births, marriages, and deaths. Tlingit hunters and warriors prayed to the spirits for success in the hunt and in battle. Spirits were also believed to

The Tlingit believed that spirits lived in the sky, the land, and the waters.

Wooden mask worn by an *ichet*

control the weather and illness. Personal guardian spirits were called *tu-kina-jek*.

Tlingit believed to have special powers were called *ichets* (spirit doctors). An ichet was a kind of priest who used magic to see the unknown, control events, or heal the sick. In some ceremonies, ichets wore robes and carved wooden masks with painted faces. Ichets sang songs and requested help from the spirits. Witches, called *nuku-sati*, were believed to have evil power that could bring harm to their villages.

Young people learned that they had two choices in life. They could seek good power and help their village or they could seek evil power and hurt their village. They learned that people would know what choice they had made by the way they lived their lives. Tlingit adults encouraged children to choose goodness. But the choice was always left to the young people. The young were expected to accept the results of their choice.

Tlingit parents arranged the marriages of their children. All Tlingit are members of either the Raven clan or Eagle clan. Ravens must marry Eagles, not other Ravens, and Eagles must marry Ravens, not other Eagles. If people married within their own clan, they could be sent away from the village forever, or even put to death. The Tlingit did not have marriage ceremonies. Marriages took place when the groom's family gave gifts to the bride's family. Divorce rarely occurred. But if the couple stopped living together, they were considered divorced. If they had children, the children always stayed with the mother because they were considered part of her clan.

The Tlingit believed every person has two spirits: one spirit during life and one spirit after death. Death spirits were believed to travel to a place in the afterlife that matched the way the person had lived while alive. Good people went to the highest heaven, called Kiwa-a. It was a place of great

This photograph of a wedding party in traditional dress was taken in 1914.

happiness. Evil people went to the lowest heaven, called Ketl-kiwa. It was a place of great unhappiness. Spirits of the dead stayed in the afterlife for a certain period of time. Then they returned to the world by being born as another person.

Some Tlingit clans **cremated** the body of the dead person.

The ashes were stored in totem poles created especially to hold the remains. A hole was carved in the back of the totem pole. The ashes were placed inside, and the hole was sealed. Some clans built small containers at the base of totem poles. The ashes were kept in these containers. After Christian missionaries arrived, however, they required the Tlingit to bury their dead in **cemeteries**.

Ceremonies were an important part of Tlingit culture. Most ceremonies were held in winter, because the Tlingit believed spirits moved closer to people in wintertime. Ceremonies were held to give thanks to spirits for a successful hunting or fishing trip, or for success in battle. Ceremonies were also held because the Tlingit believed honoring the spirits would bring them wealth and good luck.

One of the most important ceremonies was the *koolex*, or potlatch. At the potlatch, the host provided guests with food, singing, and dancing. The host and guests wore robes created especially for the potlatch. The robes were usually decorated with symbols that represented the host's clan. Potlatches

Tlingit dancers pose during a potlatch in Klukwan, Alaska.

marked important events in a person's or a family's life. These events included marriage or the birth of a child. Potlatches were also held to honor people who had died. Sometimes village chiefs held potlatches. Songs, dances, and speeches honored the chief's achievements as leader. These potlatches could last for several days, or even a few weeks. They included large feasts and gifts from the chief to the villagers.

How the Tlingit Came to Be

Raven lived on the land. He untied three bundles and let their contents float up through the smoke hole of a plankhouse. One bundle held the stars. Another bundle held the moon. The third bundle held the sun. Raven made a woman who lived under the Earth and controlled the oceans' tides. Then Raven made all the people of the Earth, including the Tlingit. He made them all speak different languages. Raven led the Tlingit under a glacier and through an ice passage to what is now the southeastern Alaska coast. They followed the present-day Nass, Stikine, and Taku rivers. Their journey ended when Raven told them they had arrived at the place where he wanted them to live.

4 · A CHANGING WORLD

The Tlingit in Alaska do not live on a reservation. They live in small communities along Alaska's coast. Tlingit in Canada live on reserves in British Columbia and Yukon Territory. Today's Tlingit have a modern lifestyle. But they maintain their language, beliefs, and unique identity as Native Americans. Children in Tlingit communities go to local schools. Adults make a living as hunters, fishers, and loggers. Others own businesses in large cities, such as Sitka and Juneau, in Alaska. Tlingit in Canada are prominent in the communities of Atlin, British Columbia, and Teslin, Yukon Territory. Many work as artists, teachers, lawyers, doctors, or for the tribal government.

In the early 1900s the governments of the United States and Canada tried to discourage the Tlingit from speaking

Mount Edgecumbe rises above the town of Sitka, Alaska.

A teacher of Tlingit heritage with two students in their classroom in Juneau, Alaska

their native language and following their traditions. Many Tlingit children were sent away from their villages to attend boarding schools. However, over time the governments of both countries passed laws to improve village and reserve life for the Tlingit. Children remained with their parents and were educated by their own people. The Tlingit were encouraged to speak their own language and to practice their traditions. In 1924 the U.S. Congress passed a law that made the Tlingit, and all Native Americans, U.S. citizens. Native people in Canada became Canadian citizens in 1951.

In 1934 Native American nations throughout the United States were granted the right to govern themselves. Since then the Tlingit in both the United States and Canada have struggled to protect their rights and their way of life. However, the governments of both nations have passed laws respecting their heritage and traditions. For example, in 1968, a U.S. court awarded the Tlingit $7.5 million for lands that had been taken from them. The lands became part of Tongass National Forest and Glacier Bay National Monument. A more recent example occurred in 2004. That year, the Supreme Court of Canada sided with the Tlingit against a company that wanted to build a highway through Tlingit territory. The ruling was important to the Tlingit. It supported their right to decide for themselves how their land and resources should be used.

In 2000 Mattel Corporation, the company that makes Barbie® dolls, began selling Northwest Coast Native American Barbie®. The doll is usually called Tlingit Barbie®. Tlingit Barbie® is not an exact representation of the Tlingit people. But the Tlingit welcomed it as a chance for Tlingit girls to play with a doll that looks like them. The doll also draws attention to the cultures of Alaska's Native people by encouraging non-Indians to learn more about them.

The Tlingit are educated at colleges and universities in Alaska, British Columbia, Yukon Territory, and other schools in the United States and Canada. In 2002 Alaska's Native people, including the Tlingit, founded Southeast Alaska's Tribal College in Juneau. This two-year college is open to Alaska's Native people, as well as non-Natives. The college's instructors are Alaska Natives. Courses are designed to meet the specific needs of the region's Native people.

The Central Council of the Tlingit and Haida Indian Tribes of Alaska represents about 26,000 Tlingit and Haida living throughout the world. The council was founded in 1939. Its

This brick government building in Juneau is decorated with Native designs and flanked by totem poles.

headquarters is located in Juneau, Alaska. The council works to help the Tlingit and Haida people achieve rights equal to those of non-Natives. It also represents the Tlingit and Haida in issues over control of the nations' traditional lands.

Every two years Juneau, Alaska, is the site of Celebration.

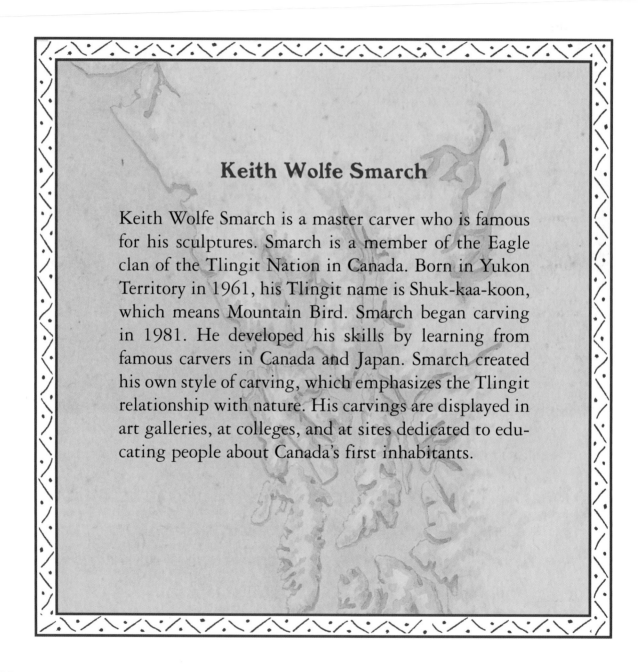

Keith Wolfe Smarch

Keith Wolfe Smarch is a master carver who is famous for his sculptures. Smarch is a member of the Eagle clan of the Tlingit Nation in Canada. Born in Yukon Territory in 1961, his Tlingit name is Shuk-kaa-koon, which means Mountain Bird. Smarch began carving in 1981. He developed his skills by learning from famous carvers in Canada and Japan. Smarch created his own style of carving, which emphasizes the Tlingit relationship with nature. His carvings are displayed in art galleries, at colleges, and at sites dedicated to educating people about Canada's first inhabitants.

Alaska Native dancers at the 2008 Celebration in Juneau

Celebration is a festival for Alaska's Native people, including the Tlingit. Families, clans, and communities sing, dance, and dress in traditional clothing to celebrate their heritage. They practice traditional arts and crafts, as well. It is one of the largest gatherings of southeastern Alaska's Native people. It is also the second-largest event held by Natives in the state of Alaska. Festivals like this help the Tlingit touch the past as they embrace the future.

· TIME LINE

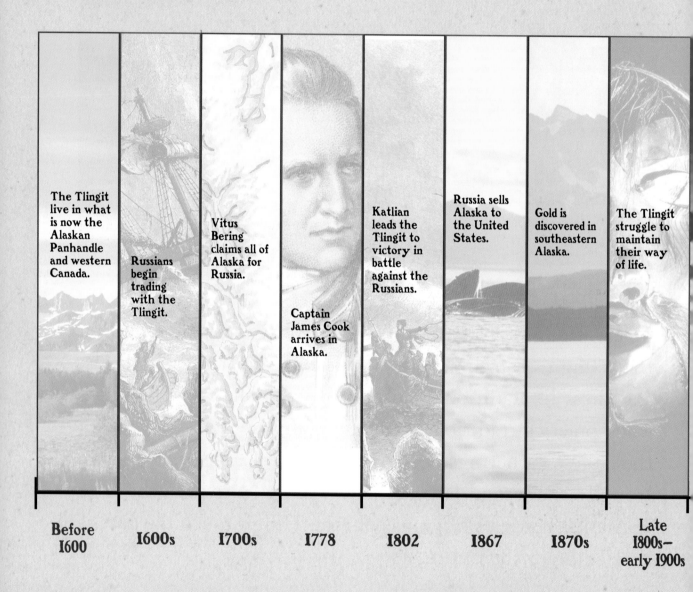

The Tlingit live in what is now the Alaskan Panhandle and western Canada.	Russians begin trading with the Tlingit.	Vitus Bering claims all of Alaska for Russia.	Captain James Cook arrives in Alaska.	Katlian leads the Tlingit to victory in battle against the Russians.	Russia sells Alaska to the United States.	Gold is discovered in southeastern Alaska.	The Tlingit struggle to maintain their way of life.
Before 1600	1600s	1700s	1778	1802	1867	1870s	Late 1800s– early 1900s

The U.S. Congress grants citizenship to all Native Americans, including the Tlingit.

The U.S. Congress passes a law to allow all Native American nations the right to govern themselves.

The Canadian Parliament passes a law granting citizenship to all Native people in Canada.

A U.S. court awards the Tlingit $7.5 million for lands taken by the U.S. government.

Mattel Corporation begins selling Tlingit Barbie®.

Southeast Alaska Tribal College is founded in Juneau.

The Supreme Court of Canada rules in favor of the Tlingit against a company that wants to build a highway through Tlingit lands.

1924   1934   1951   1968   2000   2002   2004

· GLOSSARY

ancestors: Family members who lived a long time ago.

cemeteries: Places where dead people are buried.

cremated: Burned to ashes.

game: Wild animals, including birds, that are hunted for food or sport.

missionaries: People who try to convert others to a religion.

Panhandle: The area of narrow land that extends south of Alaska.

reservations: Areas of land in the United States that are set aside for Native people to live on.

reserves: Areas of land in Canada that are set aside for Native people to live on.

rituals: Actions that are always performed in the same way as part of a religious ceremony or social custom.

· FIND OUT MORE

Books

Hancock, David. *Tlingit: Their Art and Culture*. Blaine, WA: Hancock House Publishing, 2003.

Kimmel, Eric. *The Frog Princess: A Tlingit Legend from Alaska*. New York: Holiday House, 2006.

Vanasse, Deb. *A Totem Tale*. Seattle: Sasquatch Books, 2006.

Worl, Rosita. *Celebration: Tlingit, Haida, Tsimshian Dancing on the Land*. Juneau, AK: Sealaska Heritage Institute, 2008.

Websites

Alaska Native Heritage Center
http://www.alaskanative.net
The Alaska Native Heritage Center is located in Anchorage, Alaska. You can visit in person or online to learn more about the lives of Alaska's Native people.

Alaska Native Knowledge Network
http://www.ankn.uaf.edu/index.html
This site is filled with useful information about Alaska's Natives, including the Tlingit.

The Central Council of the Tlingit and Haida Indian Tribes of Alaska
http://www.ccthita.org
This site explores current issues, events, and information on the ways the council is working to preserve Tlingit and Haida cultures.

Sealaska Heritage Institute
http://www.sealaskaheritage.org
The Sealaska Heritage Institute seeks to spread the culture and heritage of southeastern Alaska's Native nations, including the Tlingit.

Tlingit Art
http://www.indians.org/articles/tlingit_art.html
This site contains information about Tlingit art and links to sites where you can view examples of unique Tlingit creations.

About the Author

Sarah De Capua is the author of many books, including biographical, geographical, historical, and civics titles. She has always been fascinated by the earliest inhabitants of North America. In this series, she has also written *The Cherokee*, *The Cheyenne*, *The Comanche*, *The Iroquois*, *The Menominee, The Shawnee*, and *The Shoshone*. Born and raised in Connecticut, she resides in Georgia.

· INDEX

Page numbers in **boldface** are illustrations.